Chaos

Kinnari Shah

BookLeaf Publishing

India | USA | UK

Made with ❤ on the BookLeaf Publishing Platform
www.bookleafpub.in
www.bookleafpub.com

Acknowledgement

To say, 'Thank You for being my support forever' is not difficult because anyone can express that feeling through simple words.

But I sincerely want to thank my nearest one—my dear sister Nairuti Shah, who brought me on this platform to express my feelings and emotions. I am thankful to you Mumma because you have moulded me the way I am.

Thank you so much Tejas and Kavita—you both are not only siblings, though you are younger, you are my constant support. Mitva—my sister-in-law, in papa's absence, you are taking care of mumma so nicely that I could feel free from all worries about her. Devin and Zeeus—my teenage boys, who are truly my critics and inspire me to do something worthy before I get really old! Imtiyaz, my closest pal—you kept reading and listening to my poems and you are always there when I need you. Hetal, you have to bear my illogical emotions while reading these poems! Thank you for being my strength whenever I feel weak. Again, Nairu—how do I convey my gratitude for what you have provided me by making available 'BookLeaf' to me? At last, this is my tribute to my papa, my most adorable person without whom I actually forgot to live!!! Now, I am trying to live again papa... this is for "Kinnu's Papa and Papa's Kinnu".

Preface

This is my chaos. I am choosing to reveal my chaos to my readers. As someone who is the closest to heart, departs suddenly, he or she leaves the other person in some turmoil and then the chaos takes place to be understood.

My papa's sudden death shocked me and put me in a world of darkness. My sister, who is my ultimate safeguard, picked up 'Bookleaf' and provided me a reason to re-think about my life. I opened my eyes and found that this journey of words through emotions is giving me a certain type of strength. So here I am, looking forward to my readers to be with me while I am trying to come out of this 'Chaos'!

१. सफ़र

मैं ग़ज़ल हूँ, दास्ताँ हूँ
या हूँ एक कहानी!
कई किरदारों में बँटी हुई हूँ

कुछ हसीन लम्हों में या ग़म की सिलवटों से
लिपटी हुई हूँ!
अगर छू सको कभी तो सुकून हूँ
महसूस कर सको तो रूह-ए-इश्क़ हूँ
पा न सकोगे मुझको कभी जान कर भी,
तुम्हारी तन्हाइयों में,
मैं ही तो हम सफ़र हूँ!
कल रक़ीब थी,
कभी ख़्वाब या कभी ख़्वाहिश थी,
अब मंज़िल हूँ, रास्ता भी हूँ,
साथ अगर चल सको मेरे, तो हम-साया भी मैं ही हूँ

2. I just want to be myself!

No, I don't put a chain around my neck that
says I belong to you!
I love myself for my sake,
And I just belong to myself!
No, I don't want to be protected, to be
over-pampered by
false promises and fake dreams.
I like to walk on desert-sand.
I like to swim when it's over-flooded.
I like to swallow ambers.
And I just like to be myself!
No, I don't want you to love me.
I don't want you to keep waiting for me.
I don't want you to be by my side always.
You know what?
I just don't want you!

I want myself to hug me and adore me and
pamper me!
I just want to be myself!

3. इनकार

ये जो मेरे अंदर है मचल रहा,
इस शोर का मैं क्या करूँ?
नहीं, नहीं—ये न चाहिये मुझको
इस इनकार का मैं क्या करूँ?
उफान पर आई हो आवारगी अगर,
इस सैलाब का मैं क्या करूँ?
बे-लिबास हो कर सामने खड़ी है,
ऐसी नामुमकिन ख्वाहिशों का क्या करूँ?
अश्क़ दरिया न डुबो सकेंगे मुझको,
मछली-सी इस मचलन का क्या करूँ?
कश्ती लेकर चड़ जाऊँगी मौजें दरिया,
टूटी हुई इन पतवारों का क्या करूँ?
नहीं, नहीं—ये न चाहिये मुझको
इस इनकार का मैं क्या करूँ?

4. Anarchy

Two selves dwell in me.
One nefarious—the other exemplary!
Both keep conflicting all the time.
Mostly the ideal wins,
The evil sleeps silently!
Both are always mingled among the do's and
don'ts!
Both have their whys and hows!
Two selves together reside in me.
If I become submissive and polite,
The other me shouts and yells within.
If I become soft and calm,
The other one screams and denies!

One pretends to become reverent,
The other says, 'I am awful!'
You tell me,
Which one have you found?
And how does it sound?

5. ख़ालीपन

बारिश की हर बूँद के साथ
मैं तुम्हारी आहट सुनती रही।
तुम्हारे जाने के बाद जो फैली थी तन्हा,
उन साँसों को अपने अंदर भरती रही!
कुछ बिखरे तुम्हारे कपड़े समेटकर चूमती रही,
दीवारों से पूछती रही कब लौटोगे तुम?
अलमारियों से पुरानी ख़्वाहिशें निकाल कर
ख़्वाबों की शमा जलाती रही,
रुसवाई और ख़ालीपन की ज़ंजीरों को गले से
लगाकर,
तुम्हारे होंठों पर जलती सिगार-सी मैं, ज़रा-ज़रा
बिखरती रही।

6. Nothing

I have nothing to offer you.
I do not know how to please you.
My prayers disappeared,
My offerings vanished.
The flowers I plucked to welcome you,
Those are now shrivelled.
I am empty within.
I am hollow within.
Darkness inside me is abhorrent,
Though it's irrelevant.
But..
I know.
Thy name is only the remedy,
That alleviates my pain,
That soothes my strain,

So that,
I may come to you one day all by myself,
To worship you
To adore you
And just to please you!

7. पुनरुत्थान

हर शाम राख का ढेर बनती हूँ,
फिर सुबह, दिल में वो ही आग लेकर चलती हूँ।
तिनका-तिनका लेकर, आशियाना बुनती हूँ,
ये मकान है, जिसकी दीवारों में, 'घर' मैं ढूँढती हूँ।
रात के अंधेरे को, सूरज की रोशनी डुबो ही देगी,
इस हवा को मैं, अपने पंखों में भर लेती हूँ।
ये जो सामने पड़ी है, लंबी-काली, अकेली सड़क
एक-एक भर कदम,
तन्हाई के क़ाफ़िलेसे मैं जुड़ती जाती हूँ।
मुझको है मालूम तूफ़ानों से घिरी होगी मेरी
मंज़िल,
तब भी इसी राह मैं आगे बढ़ना चाहती हूँ।
हर शाम राख का ढेर बनती हूँ,
फिर सुबह, दिल में वो ही आग लेकर चलती हूँ।

8. Agony

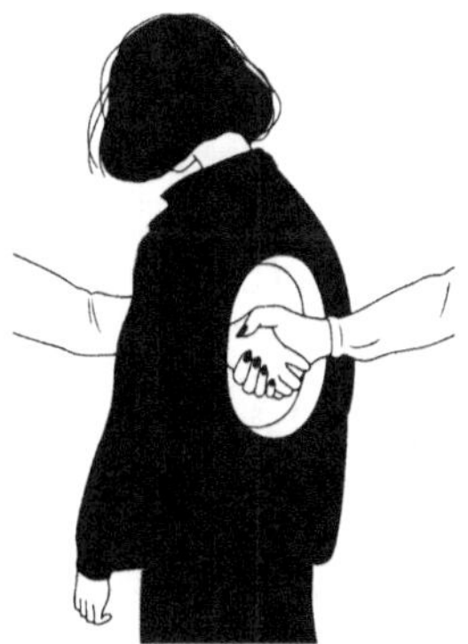

When they find you innocent and angelic,
They would immediately torment your
delicacy.
To make you obsoleted inside
To make you feel crushed inside
To make you feel disgraced,
To make you feel dejected!
Obsoleted—because you are agonised and
now tired to feel alive!
Crushed—because your beautiful heart is
injured by their words and actions!
Disgraced—because you offered them the
world of
happiness and the heaven of joy together,
And they never deserved it!

Dejected—because it's you who adored them and loved
them without knowing their ability to love
you!
So, believe me,
It's just not fair to yourself to remain
innocent and angelic always!
It's not advisable to be empathetic always!

९. शुक्राना

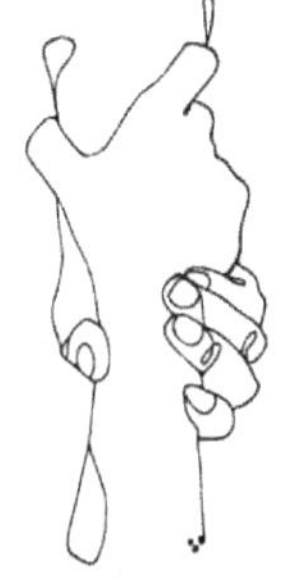

तुम्हारे वजूद पर क़ायम है
ये मेरी दुनिया
मेरे दिन रात
ये मेरे सब पल!
तुम्हारे ही होने से,
ये मैं 'मैं' हूँ
कि ये जो "मैं" अब हूँ!
वरना एक मौज काफ़ी थी,
दर्द के दरिया की
मुझको बिखेरने के लिए!
एक बवंडर ही था बहुत
इस रेत के बुत की हस्ती को मिटाने के लिए!
तुम हो, तो मैं सैलाब हूँ
कश्तियों को बहाने के लिए!
तुम हो तो मैं, एक पूरी कायनात हूँ
रब की रहमतों को खुद में ही
समेटे हुए!

10. Deflower

She cried but could not feel her tears.
The shattered glasses blinded her vision.
For the last time,
She recalled why she wanted a gold medal in
her
'Masters'?
She chose to be a doctor because she believed
in 'serve
the mankind'.
Today, she was served by few demons
disguised as men
so well, so nicely that she was bleeding
everywhere!
Poor she!

She knew how to cure injuries and wounds,
but,
She couldn't learn how to repair the
perverted souls!!
Her white coat,
Her books,
Her shoes,
Her stethoscope...
All those things got injured badly today!!
Those things once gave her an identity,
And today, they would be evidences 'at crime
scene'!!
By tomorrow,
Her friends and colleagues, her relatives....
Newspapers and advertisements...
All would bid goodbye to her!!!
Then,
Slogans and candle marches..
Posters and strikes...
Everything... everyone would bid her 'Rest In
Peace'!!!
But,
Would she be really able to 'rest in peace'?

II. खोज

वो अच्छा गाती थी।
गुनगुनाती रहती थी।
सजती थी। सँवरती थी।
खाना स्वाद बनाती थी।
अपनी गुड़िया को क़लम-किताब दिखाती थी।
बतियाती थी, लेकिन सवाल ना किसी से पूछती
थी।
एक दिन.....
उसके गानों ने वजह पूछना शुरू किया।
वो कौन थी? उसे क्या चाहिए था?
उसे सजना-सँवरना पसंद था भी?
खाने में स्वाद लाना ज़रूरी क्यों था?
क्या क़लम-किताबों की दुनिया ही हक़ीक़तों की
दुनिया
कभी बन सकती थी?

तो....
अब वो सवाल पूछने लगी है!
दहलीज़ के बाहर के आँगन से ही आसमान को
आहिस्ता से छूना
चाहती है!
अब वो सवालों के अनजान सफ़र पर जाना
चाहती है!
अपने आप को खोजना चाहती है!
अपने आप से मिलना चाहती है!

12. Hestia!

I chose to swim alone
In the deep-wide sea
When it was wild and windy
Thundery-rainy everywhere!
I chose to walk alone
On the dark-long roads
When it was dim and dull
Gusty-lonely everywhere!
I chose to fight alone
With no armours,
Weapons or warriors,
But malignity everywhere!

I never cherished roses and petals!
I never dreamed of stars and moons!
What I desired was fire and flood!
What I craved for was honor and pride!!!

13. जान अभी बाक़ी है!

मेरी आँखों में ख़्वाब और दिल में खुमार अभी
बाक़ी है।
पायलों में क़ैद और चौखट पर अटके हुए इन
कदमों में चाल अभी
बाक़ी है।
अंधेरे को पार कर के,
कल सूरज को निकलना ही होगा,
सुबह की रोशनी में मुस्कुराने वाली कलियों की
पहचान अभी बाक़ी है!
कितनी दफ़ा सूली पर चढ़ाओगे,
फिर ज़हर भरे कटोरे भी पिलाओगे?
दीवानी-पगली बुलाकर बाज़ार में दौड़ाओगे,
ज़ख्मी ज़रूर हुई है,
पर इस जिस्म में जान अभी बाक़ी है!

14. Delusion

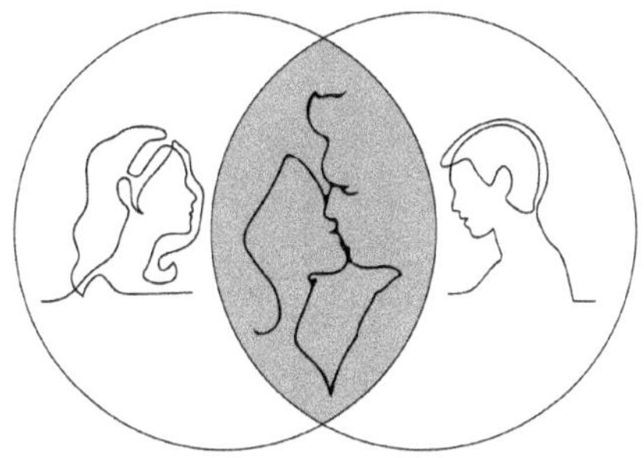

He never wanted to be the 'He'!
It was not his hobby to be known as the
'Almighty'!
But..
'She' wanted him to be so!
Because she always fantasized all her desires
to be fulfilled by 'Him'!
And for that, she was willing to cede
everything she had!
She imagined that though she had no wings,
she could fly all over the world by hiding
herself under his brave,
broad, masculine shoulders!!
She never knew that
This so-called 'her Almighty' could not be
'The God'!

The actual God was locked in Temples,
Mosques and in Churches.
Well,
The 'woman' in this poem, is poorly confused
by holding
his hand into hers to just cross this
dangerously roaring worldly ocean!!!

15. ज़ाफ़रानी चोला

ख़ाली है चोला मेरा
ख़ाली है सब कुछ मेरा!
दिल भी है ख़ाली
ख़ाली है मकान मेरा!
अब जब साहबजी आयेंगे
इस ख़ालीपन में वो ही वो सुहायेंगे!!
रंग लेंगे मुझको अपने ही रंग से,
पा लेंगे मुझको अपने ही ढंग से!
तन सफेदा-मन सफ़ेदा
जो बाक़ी था लो, कर लिया आतम भी सफ़ेदा!
अब सब ज़ाफ़रानी कर के,
वो मोहन मुस्कायेंगे!!

16. Gracious Us

I am a soothing story,
One cannot conclude.
I am a melodious poetry,
That cannot be deduced.
I am a burning desire
An aching heart might long for!
I am an ever-existing thirst
Your deserted soul might be desperate for!!
I am in You, You are in Me
That make us affably attached in this world of
chaos!!!

१7. मन मुश्ताक़ होयो

मन मुश्ताक़ होयो रे बलमवा
मन मुश्ताक़ होयो।
तोहरे इशक में,
दिन-रैन सब इक होयो।
शब भई कि अब भोर भई,
बिरहन-जोगन लोग बोलन लाग्यो,
पग पथ पर इथ-उथ जात रहे,
कहाँरी सजन दीख जावे,
कहाँरी सजन मिल जावे,
गली-डगर ना कोई अब अनजान भयो,
मन मुश्ताक़ होयो!
छोड़ी मैंने दुनियादारी,
छोड़ी मैंने यारी-दिलदारी,
बिखरी फिर भी निखरी सारी,

हो गई तोहरी दिवानी,
कुछ और अब ना सोह्यो सजनवा
मन मुश्ताक़ होयो

18. My splendid Sun

Among thousand conventional suns,
My alone-splendid sun shines so kingly!
The darkness was everywhere,
Intense like the 'Black' itself.
All suns together could not quash it,
My alone splendid sun washed it!!
Others wanted to wrap my sun
With the clouds of nescience
With the fear of ignorance
They wanted to kill my sun
With abhorrence
With intolerance
But....

Among thousand common suns,
My splendid sun shines strikingly,
It would erase their callowness
It would eat their hatred
My sun would send them the days of wine
and roses,
My sun would send them the moments of
sunshine and happiness.
My alone sun shines so differently!!

१9. बिरहन

बावरी बावरी मैं,
घूम रही थी गली-नगर, डगर-डगर।
भर केसर चुनर डाली तन पर,
खोई-खोई, रोई मैं,
सोई कंकड़-काँटों की सेज पर।
दौड़ी-दौड़ी मैं,
सुध-बुध गई, ना रही कुछ ख़बर।
ना मिले पिया, ख़ाक छानी दर-ब-दर।
भई-भई इश्कानी मैं,
चली राह अंगारों पर।
कब मिले वो पिया मेरे,
कब मिले वो जोगी मेरे,
कब मिले वो रब मेरे?
ना रहूँ मैं ऐसी बिरहन,
कैसे बनूँ मैं न्याल सुहागन?

20. 'I miss you Papa!'

That man loved me.
He simply loved me.
He just loved me so much.
His love was full of emotions..
Ocean of emotions.
He loved me so so much
That I took him for granted forever,
That I could hurt him anytime-anywhere!
If I asked for one thing,
He would buy me five things.
If I asked for something,
He would buy me 'everything'!
I used to take..take..take!!
He used to give back..back..back!!
I looked at a bird, flying in the sky,
He opened each and every possible door to
the sky,
So that I could fly high and high!

If I cried for a moment,
He would come silently, put his hand on my
head...
And would utter a single line, 'You do not
have to worry, I am here!'
Ohhhh, God...
How badly I miss that strong voice!
That warm touch of his growing-aged hand!!!
It pains me a lot.
It hurts me a lot.
It kills me every moment.
It shoots me every moment.
That man loved me abundantly
And now I am so lonely!
He gave me comfort and love,
And I took back his respect
And I rewarded him with disgrace!
Let me say sorry!
Let me be sorry!
Papa, I love you so much.
Papa, I miss you so much!!

21. जो घर था कभी, अब मकान है

पापा के जाते ही घर 'मकान' बन जाता है,
कुछ रूठ जाता है,
कुछ टूट जाता है,
गुड़िया, खिलौने और बचपन,
सब-कुछ कहीं खो जाता है।
आँगन का वो झूला अकेला रह जाता है,
पापा के पाँवों का झूला अब नहीं मिलने वाला है!
सीधे लगते थे जो सारे रास्ते,
पापा के जाते ही टेढ़े-सूने दिखने लगते हैं।
सामने दिखा करती थी जो मंज़िल,
वो नज़रों से ओझल होने लगती है।
पापा के जाते ही,
जो घर था,
वो 'मकान' बनने लगता है।

22. .... तो मेरे साथ चलो

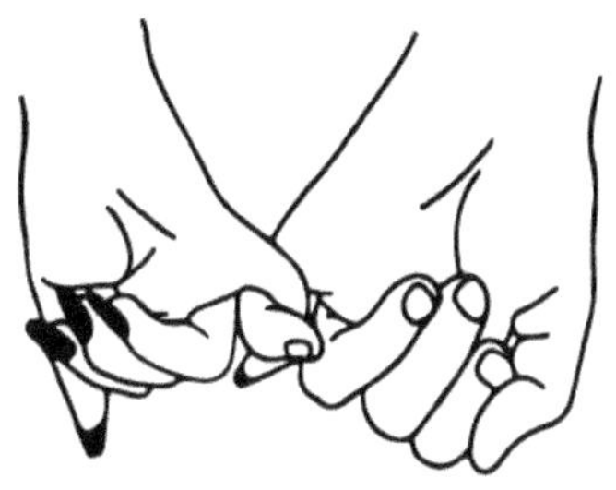

कुछ कहूँ या ख़ामोश रहूँ
तुम समझ सको तो सुनो।
क़समें-वादे और साथ निभाने के
कुछ दौर होते हैं,
वो ख़त्म हो,
तब भी,
चल सको तो मेरे साथ चलो।
कश्तियाँ किनारों पर लगने से पहले,
कभी दरिया में डूबती भी है,
भँवर पर फँसे हो जब,
तब साथ कूद सको,
तो चलो।
इश्क़-ए-गुनाह मान लिया है मैंने,
सज़ा जो मिले वो हो अगर क़ुबूल,
तो मेरे साथ चलो।
कुछ कहूँ या ख़ामोश रहूँ
तुम समझ सको तो सुनो।

जल रहा है ये वजूद मेरा
बिखरती राख जो बटोर सको,
तो मेरे साथ चलो।

23. मछली को चाँद की ख्वाहिश

समंदर की मछली को चाँद की ख्वाहिश थी,
पर बिना पानी वो जी कैसे सकती थी?
उसके आँगन में चाँद हर रात उतरता था,
किस से कहती?
वो तो उसे छू तक नहीं सकती थी।
आँगन के चाँद को वो तकती रहती थी,
पानी के बुलबुलों से उसे सहलाया करती थी,
रात चलती रहती थी,
मछली मचलती रहती थी।
कैसे सोचती?
सुबह के आते ही चाँद को तो जाना होगा,
उजाले से आँगन भर जायेगा,
पर दिल न अब रोशन रहेगा,
चाँद को वो कहाँ जा कर लिपट सकती थी?

24. I Shall Meet You There.

I will walk through thorns,
And shall meet you there,
Where the radiant Sun shines,
And stars play.
I will give you my heart,
And then stay in rest!
I will speak through music,
And shall meet you there,
Where the valley echos,
And flowers play.
I will offer you my heart,
And then stay in rest!

I will rise through fire,
And shall meet you there,
Where the blaze is intense,
And embers play.
I will cede my heart,
And then stay in rest!